TRUE or
FALSE?

These objects helped
kill 12 people in
Tokyo, Japan.

TRUE!

A plastic bag full of deadly sarin gas was hidden inside a newspaper on a Tokyo subway. The umbrella tip was used to puncture the bag. That released the poison and killed 12 passengers.

This is a real example of bioterrorism. Bioterrorism involves the use of a weapon made of a biological material to hurt or kill people. Want to find out more? Read on.

Book design Red Herring Design/NYC

Library of Congress Cataloging-in-Publication Data
Rudy, Lisa Jo, 1960–
Bioterror : deadly invisible weapons /
by Lisa Jo Rudy. 1960–
p. cm. – (24/7: science behind the scenes)
Includes bibliographical references and index.
ISBN-13: 978-0-531-12080-4 (lib. bdg.)   978-0-531-18742-5 (pbk.)
ISBN-10: 0-531-12080-5 (lib. bdg.)   0-531-18742-X (pbk.)
1. Biological warfare—Juvenile literature. 2. Biological weapons—
Juvenile literature. 3. Bioterrorism—Juvenile literature I. Title.
UG447.8.R74 2007
363.325'3—dc22   2007015812

BIOTERROR

Deadly Invisible Weapons

Lisa Jo Rudy

WARNING: The cases described in this book are real. And they all involve invisible poisons that can kill anyone in their paths.

Franklin Watts
An Imprint of Scholastic Inc.
New York • Toronto • London • Auckland • Sydney
Mexico City • New Delhi • Hong Kong
Danbury, Connecticut

CONTENTS

THE 411

↱ Read this section to learn how bioterror experts catch the bad guys.

8
OVERHEARD
Bioterror Talk

10
SEE FOR YOURSELF
Four Deadly Bioweapons

12
WHO'S WHO?
The Bioterror Team

Find out about some of the world's scariest bioterror attacks.

Sarin gas is released in the subways in Tokyo, Japan.

15 Case #1:
Terror in the Tokyo Subway
A religious cult releases deadly poison underground. Twelve people die. How did it happen—and why?

25 Case #2:
Mystery in a Small Oregon Town
More than 750 people get violently ill from food poisoning. Is it an accident—or a bioterrorist attack?

Salad bars in Oregon sent hundreds to the hospital.

E
LE SCHOOL
PARK NJ 08852

SENATOR LEAHY
433 RUSSELL SENATE OF
BUILDING
WASHINGTON D.C. 20510-

35

520+4502

Case #3:
Murder by U.S. Mail
Someone has sent letters containing a lethal poison. Who's behind this bioterrorism?

In fall 2001, deadly anthrax was sent to some VIPs.

THE DOWNLOAD

Here's even more amazing stuff about bioterrorism.

44 *FLASHBACK*
Key Dates in Bioterror

RIPPED FROM THE HEADLINES **46**
In the News

48 *REAL STUFF*
Bioterror Safety: A Guide

The Bioterror Expert's Toolbox **50**

52 *CAREERS*
Help Wanted: Microbiologist

YELLOW PAGES

56 RESOURCES

59 DICTIONARY

62 INDEX

64 AUTHOR'S NOTE

Say a dozen people from an office building are rushed to the hospital. They are violently ill. But even the doctors can't figure out why.

THE 411

That's a job for microbiologists. They'll figure out what's causing the illness. If they determine that a biological or chemical weapon is involved, they'll call in the bioterror experts.

IN THIS SECTION:

▶ how microbiologists really talk;
▶ the most dangerous bioweapons in the world;
▶ and who else is on the bioterror team.

Bioterror Talk

Microbiologists and other people who fight bioterrorism have their own way of talking. Find out what their vocabulary means.

FBI
(ef-bee-EYE) the federal agency that investigates terrorism and other criminal activities; it's short for *Federal Bureau of Investigation*.

Somebody, call the **FBI**. There's been an act of **terrorism** using a deadly **bioweapon**.

terrorism
(TAIR-uhr-ih-zuhm) an act of violence against people for the purpose of creating confusion and fear. It's often used to protest a country's politics.

bioweapon
(BYE-oh-WEH-puhn) a weapon that kills or injures through the use of poisons, germs, or nerve gas

Get the **microbiology** team in here — fast. There's an envelope with some **spores** we need to check out.

microbiology
(MYE-kro-bye-OL-uh-jee) the study of living things too small to be seen without a microscope

spores
(spohrz) tiny, microscopic germs that can reproduce under the right conditions

Now, let's not jump to any conclusions. We don't know that this is an attack on **civilians**. It could just be just some harmless **bacteria**.

Say What?

Here's some other lingo experts might use on the job.

civilians
(si-VIL-yuhnz) people who are not members of the armed forces; ordinary citizens

bacteria
(bak-TEER-ee-ah) tiny, single-celled life-forms found in the air, soil, and water. Some bacteria are harmless; others can cause terrible diseases.

biowarrior
(BYE-oh-WOR-ee-ur) a person who combats bioterror
"No one knows more about the anthrax attack than she does— she's a real biowarrior."

nerve gas
(nurv gahs) a gas that attacks the brain and nervous system
"Nerve gas was used during World War I."

vaccine
(vak-SEEN) an injection given to prevent a specific illness
"The smallpox vaccine was so successful that no one gets sick with smallpox anymore."

Careful, it's a deadly **virus**! It's probably a **bioterror** agent.

virus
(VYE-ruhs) a tiny substance that can cause disease

bioterror
(BYE-oh-TAIR-ur) a terrorist attack using biological or chemical weapons

WMD
(DUH-bul-yoo-em-dee) bioweapons like nerve gas or anthrax that can kill many people at once; it's short for *weapons of mass destruction.*
"If they have any WMD, then they are a serious threat to our safety."

Four Deadly Bioweapons

Here are some deadly biological and chemical weapons that have been used in the past.

Bioagent	What Is It?	Symptoms
ANTHRAX 	Anthrax is a bacterial disease. It occurs in animals like sheep and goats. It's rare in humans.	Blisters, stomachache, and diarrhea. It can be fatal.
SALMONELLA 	Salmonella is a natural bacteria found in uncooked foods like eggs and chicken.	Stomachache, nausea, vomiting, and diarrhea. It is rarely fatal.
SARIN 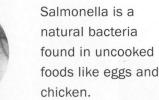	Sarin is a chemical made in a lab. It's similar to **pesticides**. Humans get sick by breathing it in.	Runny nose, rapid heartbeat, confusion, weakness, and paralysis. A small amount can be deadly.
SMALLPOX 	Smallpox is a deadly virus that spreads from contact with an infected person.	Early symptoms are like the flu. Then you get red spots. Up to 35% of smallpox victims die.

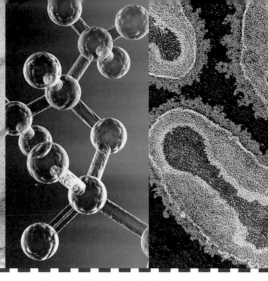

Cure	Bioweapon Potential	Real Cases
Some forms of anthrax can be cured with **antibiotics**.	Anthrax can be turned into a powder. It's deadly if you touch or inhale it.	Anthrax was used as a bioweapon in 2001. It was sent in letters. Five people died.
People usually get over salmonella by themselves. It can also be treated with antibiotics.	It's fairly easy to find salmonella. It's more difficult to put it into the food supply.	Salmonella was used as a bioweapon in Oregon during the 1980s. Hundreds got sick, but no one died.
There is treatment for sarin, but it must be taken soon after exposure.	It's fairly easy for a chemist to make sarin liquid. It's hard to make sarin gas.	Sarin gas was used as a bioweapon twice in Japan in the 1990s. It killed 19 and injured many more.
There is a vaccine to prevent smallpox. It works so well that the disease was eliminated in 1979.	Smallpox can be sprayed into the air. It can also be carried by someone who has been infected.	Recently, both Russia and Serbia have been accused of producing the smallpox virus in secret labs.

The Bioterror Team

These days, a lot of people are keeping an eye out for bioterrorism.

CDC OFFICIALS
These experts investigate health emergencies. They work with local health officials to determine whether an event was a bioterror attack. If it was, they pass their evidence to microforensics experts.

LOCAL HEALTH OFFICIALS
They figure out exactly what is causing a health problem. They're also in charge of deciding whether something is an act of bioterror or just a natural outbreak of disease.

FBI AGENTS
They study crime scenes carefully, question suspects, and examine evidence. They are in charge of catching the terrorists who commit bioterror attacks.

VIROLOGISTS
They study how viruses work, how they make people sick, and how they spread. They help develop treatments and vaccines.

INTERPOL AGENTS
They work with the FBI to find bioterrorists around the world. Interpol serves 186 countries around the world.

MICROFORENSICS EXPERTS
They use microscopes and high-tech equipment to analyze evidence of a biological attack. They find out where the bioweapon comes from. And they pass information on to agents at the FBI.

TRUE-LIFE
CASE FILES!

24 hours a day, 7 days a week, 365 days a year, experts are working to protect people from acts of bioterror.

IN THIS SECTION:

- ► tracking a cult that gassed 12 people in the Tokyo subway;
- ► solving 751 mysterious cases of food poisoning in Oregon;
- ► and hunting terrorists who killed with anthrax!

24/7 Science Behind the Scenes

How do bioterror experts get the job done?

Each of the cases you're about to read is very different. But the steps the experts followed are similar. Scientists and other professionals use a specific process to figure out, or diagnose, what's wrong in a situation. You can follow this process as you read the case studies. Keep an eye out for the icons below.

THE QUESTION
At the beginning of each case, the bioterror experts ask **one or two main questions** about the case they're trying to solve.

THE EVIDENCE
The next step is to **gather and analyze evidence**. The experts gather as much information as they can. Then they study it and figure out what it means.

THE CONCLUSION
Along the way, they come up with theories about what may have happened. They test these theories in a lab. Do the results back up the theory? If so, they've **reached the conclusion**.

Tokyo, Japan
March 20, 1995
7:48 A.M.

Terror in the Tokyo Subway

A religious cult releases deadly poison underground. Twelve people die. How did it happen— and why?

Rush-Hour Horror!

March 20, 1995, begins as an ordinary Monday in Tokyo. But it is anything but that.

On the morning of the attacks, the subway cars in Tokyo were so crowded it was impossible to move.

At 7:30 A.M. on March 20, 1995, it was the peak of the Monday morning rush hour in Tokyo, Japan.

No one noticed when Ikuo Hayashi boarded a car on the Chiyoda line at 7:48. He wore a surgical mask. In Japan, this is common during flu season.

What wasn't common was the plastic bag Hayashi was carrying. It was wrapped in newspaper. And inside it was one liter (34 oz) of sarin gas. A small bit of sarin gas can kill an adult.

Hayashi was also carrying an umbrella. The tip had been sharpened like a dart.

As the train pulled into a station, Hayashi dropped the plastic bag and stabbed it several times with the tip of the umbrella.

When the train doors opened, Hayashi got off. Outside, he climbed into a waiting car driven by Tomomitsu Niimi.

Back inside the Chiyoda subway car, riders began to feel the effects of the leaking sarin gas. Two collapsed. By the end of the day, they were both dead.

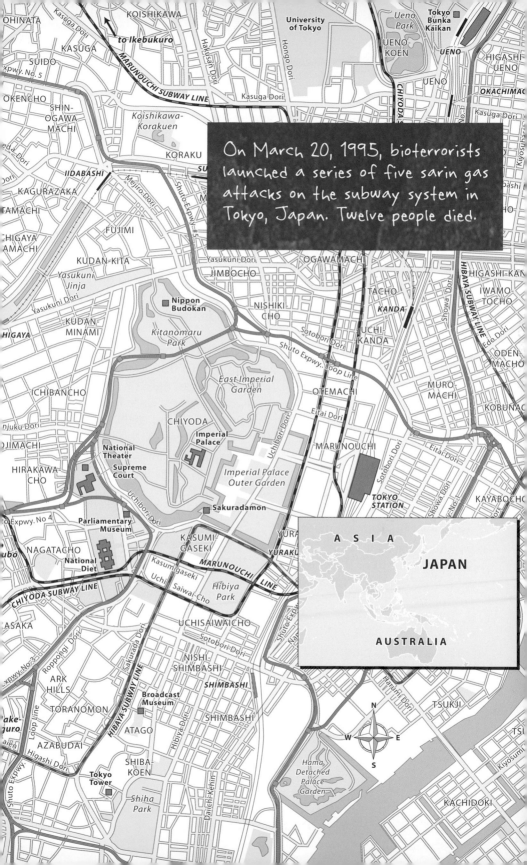

On March 20, 1995, bioterrorists launched a series of five sarin gas attacks on the subway system in Tokyo, Japan. Twelve people died.

WHAT IS SARIN GAS?

The deadly chemical used in the Tokyo subway attacks is related to some pesticides.

Sarin is a deadly chemical that attacks the human nervous system. Your nervous system controls everything you do with your body.

Sarin can stop your heart, stop your breathing, or leave you blind. It's so powerful that a very small amount can kill a human.

Discovered in Germany

Sarin is similar to some chemicals used to kill insects. It was discovered in 1938 by two German scientists. The following year, the German Army began producing sarin as a bioweapon to use against the U.S. in World War II (1939–1945).

The Germans planned to fire shells filled with sarin gas at their enemies. But they changed their minds. They realized that U.S. scientists would develop their own chemical weapons to use against Germany.

Sarin Used by Iraq

In 1980, Iraq launched sarin gas attacks against Iran. The two countries were fighting a war that lasted eight years.

Then in 1988, the Iraq government, led by Saddam Hussein, used sarin in attacks against its own people in the city of Halabja. An estimated 5,000 people died.

The United Nations banned the production of sarin gas in 1993. More than 160 countries around the globe signed the bill outlawing this deadly chemical weapon.

But two years later, terrorists attacked the Tokyo subway system with sarin gas.

Five Attacks—12 Dead!

The subway terrorists launch five sarin gas attacks at the same time.

Hayashi and Niimi weren't the only attackers that morning. In all, there were five identical sarin gas attacks in the Tokyo subway system.

While Hayashi and Niimi hit the Chiyoda line, four other pairs of killers were attacking other subway lines. These men also placed plastic bags of sarin gas in subway cars and punctured them with umbrellas.

These men were bioterrorists. This means they used biological or chemical weapons to hurt civilians.

On the Ogikubo-bound line, two passengers exposed to the deadly gas had trouble breathing. They collapsed before the train was taken out of service. One died.

On the Ikebukuro-bound line, the bag of sarin gas had barely been punctured. Some passengers complained of a bad smell. The train was searched, but the sarin wasn't found. The floor was mopped, and the train kept going. It stayed in service for nearly two hours more. Luckily, no one died.

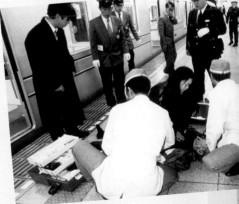

Medical workers treating the victims of the sarin attack. There were five separate sarin attacks that morning.

On the Naka-Meguro-bound line, a passenger kicked the leaking bag of sarin out of the subway car and onto the crowded subway platform. Four people on the platform died. Meanwhile, the train continued. When it finally stopped, the doors opened, and two people collapsed onto the platform. Four passengers died.

On the departing Naka-Meguro line, riders began to panic. Several were removed from the train and taken to a nearby hospital. But the train continued for several more stations before it was **evacuated**. Amazingly, only one person died.

It was a chaotic scene outside the Tokyo subway. Police and medical workers rushed to help the victims.

In all, 12 people died in the five sarin gas bioattacks. Hospitals treated more than 5,500 patients. Some temporarily lost their eyesight. Others had trouble breathing or experienced nose bleeds, nausea, and vomiting.

The attacks had tragic consequences. But they also showed how difficult it is to commit acts of terrorism using sarin gas.

Hunting for the Killers

Police are determined to find the terrorists who killed 12 people in the Tokyo subway.

Japanese police began their hunt for the Tokyo sarin gas killers. The police needed to answer these questions: Who carried out the attacks? And why did they do it?

Crime scene investigators put on protective suits and gas masks. They went into the subway cars. They found the plastic bags left by the attackers. Handling them with great care, they sent them to the lab to be tested.

Forensics experts **analyzed** the liquid in the plastic bags. Indeed, the bags had been full of deadly sarin gas.

There had been only one previous case of sarin poisoning in Japan. It had happened the year before in the city of Matsumoto. In that attack, seven people had been killed.

Officials wore biohazard suits to protect themselves as they investigated the sarin attacks.

Investigators had taken soil samples from the poisoned area in Matsumoto. Now they compared the sarin from the subway to the sarin from Matsumoto. It was a match! The deadly gas is extremely difficult to make. So

After the sarin attacks, the subway stations were thoroughly cleaned.

it seemed likely that the same killers had committed both crimes.

Police suspected that a **cult** called Aum Shinrikyo was responsible for the Matsumoto killings. But they hadn't been able to prove it. Now they would try again.

Busting the Bad Guys

Police shift their attention to the Aum Shinrikyo cult.

Aum Shinrikyo had started as an ordinary religious organization. But over time, the group began acting suspiciously. Members of Aum were suspected of kidnapping and murder. They were accused of collecting weapons and forcing members to stay in the cult against their will.

Two days after the Tokyo subway attack, 2,500 police raided Aum buildings around Japan.

Inside, they found many chemicals, including an insect poison that resembled sarin. They found a full chemical plant. Pipes led from the plant to labs filled with bottles and equipment. The police took away samples of all the chemicals. Forensics experts discovered that some of the samples were deadly sarin.

Shoko Asahara was the leader of the Aum Shinrikyo cult.

Over the next week, more evidence was collected. At Aum headquarters near Mount Fuji, police found explosives and bioterror weapons, including deadly anthrax and **Ebola**.

The police concluded that members of Aum Shinrikyo had committed the five Tokyo subway attacks that killed 12 people.

Within six weeks, the police arrested more than 150 members of Aum. In response, Shoko Asahara, the cult's leader, threatened to cause more disasters. The government of Japan stockpiled treatments for nerve gas—just in case the threats were real!

The Final Attacks

Aum's reign of terror comes to an end.

Takaji Kunimatsu, head of the National Police Agency in Japan, investigated the involvement of Aum Shinrikyo in the Tokyo attacks. During this investigation, he was shot and seriously injured in front of his house.

Several months later, on May 5, a burning paper bag was discovered in Tokyo's busiest subway station. It contained a poison bomb that could have killed 20,000 passengers.

Several more poison bombs were found in the subways during the next few weeks. But no passengers were hurt or killed.

Eventually, the police arrested Asahara. He was charged with 23 counts of murder and sentenced to death for the sarin gas attacks. Several other cult members were also sentenced to death.

Cult members never explained the motive for the attacks.

Many people saw the attack in Tokyo and thought: "This could happen anywhere." And it could. But it's important to remember that bioterrorism is not easy, and it's not cheap. Aum spent $30 million on their plans. They had some top scientists. But they still had a hard time making effective bioweapons. 24/7

In the next case, is another cult to blame for poisoning 750 people in rural Oregon?

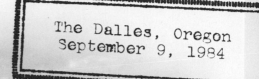

The Dalles, Oregon
September 9, 1984

Mystery in a Small Oregon Town

More than 750 people get violently ill from food poisoning. Is it an accident—or a bioterrorist attack?

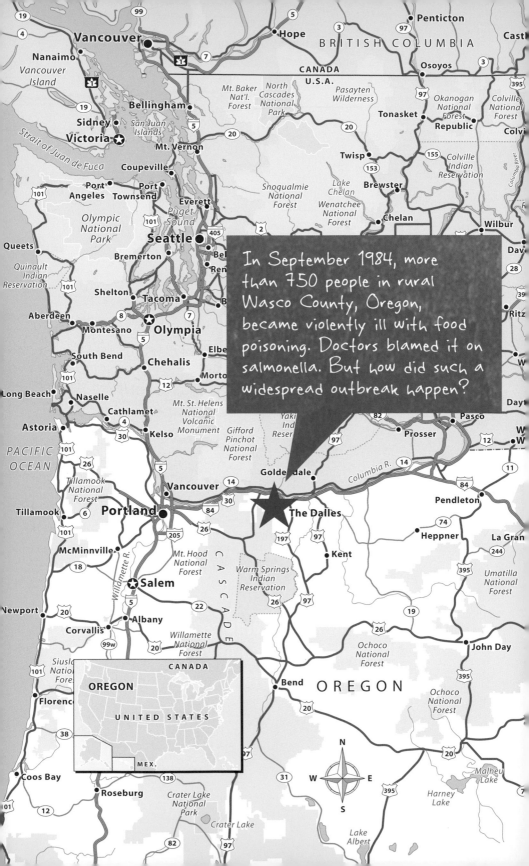

In September 1984, more than 750 people in rural Wasco County, Oregon, became violently ill with food poisoning. Doctors blamed it on salmonella. But how did such a widespread outbreak happen?

A Small-Town Epidemic

Dozens of people check into an Oregon hospital with food poisoning. Is it a coincidence—or a plot?

On the night of September 9, 1984, Daniel Erickson was admitted to the only hospital in the small town of The Dalles, Oregon. He was complaining of intense stomach cramps, nausea, and high fever.

His friends Dave and Sandy Luntgens were also sick. Earlier that day, all three had eaten at the Shakey's Pizza restaurant that the Luntgens couple owned. Soon, 13 of the restaurant's employees and dozens of customers became violently ill.

The Dalles is a small town of just 11,000 people along the Columbia River in Wasco County, Oregon. The mystery illness seemed to spread all over town. Before long, patients who had eaten in four different local restaurants checked into the hospital with identical symptoms.

Health experts at Mid-Columbia Medical Center found that the cause of illness was salmonella. Salmonella is a bacteria that occurs naturally. At first, doctors assumed the

This microbiologist is studying the salmonella bacteria. It is usually found in raw and undercooked foods.

outbreak of food poisoning was an accident. They gave patients antibiotics to cure the illness and sent them home.

Erickson and the Luntgenses soon recovered, and things went back to normal in The Dalles. At least for a few days . . .

WHAT IS SALMONELLA?

This bacteria exists naturally in many foods.

Salmonella is a bacteria that exists naturally in many raw foods, including milk, seafood, and some vegetables. You can get salmonella if you eat raw eggs or undercooked chicken. About 40,000 cases of salmonella happen every year in the U.S.

Salmonella is rarely fatal. Most often, infected people get diarrhea, abdominal cramps, and fever. Other symptoms include chills, headache, and nausea.

Most people with salmonella recover without treatment and may never see a doctor. However, salmonella infections are particularly dangerous for young children, the elderly, and people with damaged immune systems.

Avoiding Salmonella

The best way to avoid salmonella is to make sure all foods are thoroughly washed and cooked. Wash your hands carefully after handling raw food. Also, use soap and hot water to clean cutting boards, countertops, and other places where food is prepared.

A Second Attack of Salmonella

Food poisoning returns to The Dalles. But this time, hundreds of people are sickened.

On September 21, a second wave of illness hit Wasco County. This time, so many people got sick that every hospital bed was filled with salmonella victims. They had violent stomach cramps, chills, and diarrhea. Some were dizzy and had nosebleeds.

There weren't enough hospital rooms, so patients were kept on beds in crowded hallways. They grew afraid and angry. Some got violent and yelled at the nurses. The doctors could barely treat them all.

In all, more than 1,000 people who lived in Wasco County entered the hospital. That was more than 10 percent of the population of the entire town. Doctors confirmed 751 cases of salmonella. Surprisingly, the victims had eaten at 10 different restaurants. There were 38 restaurants in the entire town.

Doctors wondered how the salmonella outbreak could be so widespread. Was it a coincidence that all 10 restaurants made people sick? Or was there a more troubling explanation?

Hospital workers in Wasco County rushed to treat all the salmonella victims. But the hospital didn't have enough beds, so some patients were treated in the hallways.

Investigators Try to Solve the Case

Local doctors call in experts from the CDC.

The first break in the case came because of nurse Carla Chamberlain.

Chamberlain worked at the local hospital. As soon as the second wave of salmonella hit, she began interviewing patients to find out what they had eaten the previous three days.

Chamberlain quickly realized that most of the patients had eaten at salad bars in one of the 10 restaurants. Immediately, health officials asked all local restaurants to close their salad bars.

Federal investigators from the Food and Drug Administration (**FDA**) visited the 10

Most of the people who had gotten sick in Wasco had eaten at salad bars. So investigators tested the food there first.

restaurants. They checked to see if refrigerated items like potato salad or blue cheese dressing had gone bad. They checked the restaurants' water supply, looking for **contamination**. But they found nothing that would explain 751 cases of salmonella.

Dr. John Livengood and a team of experts from the Centers for Disease Control and Prevention (**CDC**) in Atlanta also came to Oregon to help. They found that the type of salmonella making people sick was very unusual.

Livengood started to wonder if this was a case of bioterrorism. But no person or group had claimed responsibility for the outbreak. And the CDC team couldn't find anyone who wanted to hurt the restaurants or their customers. So Livengood concluded that the outbreak was accidental.

Fortunately, no one else got sick from salmonella. The investigators left town. And things got back to normal—sort of.

People in Wasco County were still worried. Many believed that the salmonella attacks were no accident. And they thought they knew who was responsible.

The Cult of Rajneesh

A religious leader and his 7,000 followers come under suspicion for the salmonella attacks.

Bhagwan Shree Rajneesh was the leader of a religious cult that settled in Oregon.

Three years before the salmonella attacks, a new resident came to town. He was known as Bhagwan Shree Rajneesh. He was also sometimes called Osho. And he was the leader of his own religious cult of 7,000 followers.

Rajneesh had bought a 100-acre (40-ha) ranch called The Big Muddy. There, the cult turned their community into a city named Rajneeshpuram. They created their own police force. They collected weapons. And they were voted onto the city council of the nearby town of Antelope.

Shortly before the first salmonella outbreak, two county commissioners visited Osho's ranch to investigate the compound. Both suddenly became ill with salmonella-like symptoms. And after the visit, they received threats in the mail.

News of the poisoning and the threats got out. Many residents of Wasco County became suspicious of the cult—and afraid of what cult members might do. "For us, in small-town America, it was overwhelming," said Karen LeBreton. She was Wasco County's deputy clerk.

The Bioterrorists Confess!

The Rajneesh cult admits its plan to poison local voters with salmonella.

Members of the Rajneesh cult at prayer.

It would take two years to discover the truth.

By 1986 Osho was losing control of his cult. After some fights within the group, he called the police. He accused two members of criminal activity. He said they had tried to poison the county water supply with salmonella.

Wasco County Sheriff Art Labrousse headed the local deputy force of 13. Labrousse called in federal authorities to help.

They searched the cult's ranch. There, they found a hidden lab that had been used to grow germs. They found traces of the same salmonella that had been used to poison the salad bars two years before!

Labrousse and his team also found germs that were even more dangerous than salmonella. These included deadly **typhoid fever** and **tularemia**.

Members of the cult began to confess. Yes, they had planned to contaminate The Dalles water supply. They wanted the locals to become too sick to vote in upcoming county elections. They wanted their own candidates to win. The salmonella in the salad bars was just a first test.

33

More than 20 cult members were charged with crimes. Two of them spent four years in prison for the salmonella poisoning. Osho didn't go to jail, but he paid a $400,000 fine and was forced to leave the U.S.

Many local residents had suffered because of the cult's attacks. Restaurant owner Dave Luntgens said he lost nearly $500,000 in sales and insurance claims when 400 customers at his Shakey's Pizza restaurant became sick.

"We lived with fear on a daily basis," said Wasco County clerk Sue Proffitt. "We understand in The Dalles how bioterrorism can happen." 24/7

A sample of salmonella growing in a laboratory. The purple stuff is called agar. It's a substance used for growing bacteria.

In this case, a cult poisoned more than 750 townspeople to try to win a local election. In the next case, who's to blame for killing five innocent people with deadly anthrax?

New York, Washington, D.C.,
and Florida
September-October, 2001

Murder by U.S. Mail

Someone has sent letters
containing a lethal poison. Who's
behind this bioterrorism?

Death in a White Envelope

Five people die after handling letters containing a mysterious powder. But who sent them?

On September 11, 2001, Al Qaeda terrorists flew two airplanes into New York City's World Trade Center towers. Both 110-story buildings collapsed, killing thousands of people. The terrorists also flew a plane into the Pentagon in Washington, D.C. Another plane piloted by terrorists crashed in a field in Pennsylvania.

Many Americans feared that more terrorist attacks would happen soon. And 10 days later, their fears seemed to be realized. Johanna Huden, who worked at the *New York Post* newspaper, noticed a big red bump on her finger. Two days later, her finger began to swell and turned black. She felt like she had the flu.

Huden went to the hospital. Tests showed that she had anthrax. Anthrax is a rare disease, usually spread by infected farm animals. Huden was given the drug Cipro, which cured her. But doctors wondered: How did she catch anthrax in the middle of New York City?

Then, there were more victims. On October 5, a magazine photo editor in

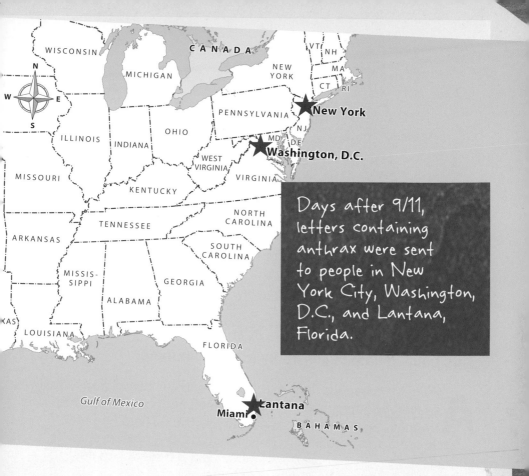

Days after 9/11, letters containing anthrax were sent to people in New York City, Washington, D.C., and Lantana, Florida.

Lantana, Florida, named Robert Stevens died. Soon, four more people died. In all, more than 20 people became infected with anthrax.

Police and FBI agents began to investigate. They learned that everyone who caught anthrax had opened letters containing a powder. Lab tests showed that the powder was anthrax bacteria.

This is one of the letters that contained anthrax. It was sent to an editor at the *New York Post* newspaper.

EDITOR
NEW YORK POST
1211 AVE. OF THE AMERICA
NEW YORK NY 10036

It was the second terrorist attack in the U.S. in just one month. Who was sending the anthrax, the FBI agents wondered? And how many more innocent people would die?

WHAT IS ANTHRAX?

This deadly disease normally infects animals.

Anthrax is a serious illness caused by a bacteria. Normally, only animals catch it. Anthrax is rare in humans.

It's possible for people to get anthrax by eating undercooked meat from animals with anthrax. Or they can get it by breathing in anthrax spores from infected animals' products—like wool.

But that's extremely rare.

Anthrax as a Weapon

Even before World War II (1939–1945), governments began developing anthrax to use as a bioweapon. The U.S. and Britain made and tested anthrax weapons. And many other nations did, too.

In the Soviet Union in 1979, more than 60 people died when a bioweapons factory accidentally released anthrax powder into the air. The Soviets had made hundreds of tons of anthrax to use as a bioweapon in case of war.

A Cure for Anthrax?

Some types of anthrax can be cured, but only if those infected are treated immediately. They can take an antibiotic like Cipro, which kills anthrax.

Scientists are also working on vaccines that prevent people from catching anthrax. In 2004, President George W. Bush signed a law giving billions of dollars to help create 75 million doses of anthrax vaccine. So far, the vaccine is only for people who have been exposed to the disease.

Poison Pen Pal

The anthrax letters lead the FBI to suspect a scientist is behind the attacks.

The FBI began its investigation by studying the poisoned letters.

THE EVIDENCE

One of the letters was mailed to Tom Brokaw in New York City. Brokaw was a famous journalist and anchor of the *NBC Nightly News*. His assistant had opened the letter and caught anthrax—though she later recovered.

Other letters were sent to two U.S. senators in Washington, D.C. They both came from this address: 4th Grade, Greendale School, Franklin Park, NJ 08852.

When FBI investigators tried to find the Greendale School, they found there was no such place.

The writing was in large block letters, as if a child had written the notes. But FBI **profilers** knew an adult had written them. Profilers are agents who study past cases to figure out who committed new crimes. They came up with a theory about the anthrax terrorist.

09-11-01
THIS IS NEXT
TAKE PENACILIN NOW

DEATH TO AMERICA
DEATH TO ISRAEL

ALLAH IS GREAT

Tom Brokaw, a famous journalist at NBC, also received an envelope containing anthrax. This note was inside.

The suspect was probably a man who had worked in a lab with hazardous materials. He was a scientist who had access to anthrax and knew how to refine it into a deadly powder. He might have been in the military. He was angry. And he probably lived alone.

The Anthrax Letters: A Cold Case?

More than five years after the attacks, no one has been arrested for the crime.

Over the past five years, the FBI and other investigators traveled to six continents. They interviewed more than 9,000 people. They followed 53,000 leads. They did hundreds of searches. But they haven't made a single arrest in the anthrax case.

Still, the FBI is working to solve the crime. "Today, the FBI's commitment to solving this case is undiminished," said Joseph Persichini. He's the acting assistant director of the FBI's Washington office.

"No arrests have been made," Persichini

said. "But the dedicated investigators who have worked tirelessly on this case . . . continue to go the extra mile in pursuit of every lead."

There's a huge reward for any person who helps the FBI catch the anthrax killer. But some people think the case will never be solved.

The good news is that the anthrax attacks stopped almost as soon as they started—way back in 2001. **24/7**

Workers cleaned up the Florida offices where the photo editor, Robert Stevens, received a deadly letter.

ANTHRAX FINGERPRINTS

Let's say some microbiologists have a sample of anthrax. How do they learn about it?

They study the anthrax sample's DNA.
There are at least 89 different types—or strains—of anthrax. And each strain has its own **DNA**. DNA is the biological information almost every living thing carries in its cells. So microbiologists can determine what strain of anthrax a sample is by examining its DNA.

They look for agar in the anthrax sample.
When chemists make anthrax in a lab, they grow it in a goo called **agar**. Microbiologists use powerful microscopes to search for tiny bits of agar on anthrax spores. If they find it, they know the anthrax is made in a laboratory—not scraped off a sheep!

They examine the water in the anthrax sample.
The water used to make the anthrax sample can tell scientists where the anthrax was made. How? Microbiologists study the chemical makeup of the water. They can pinpoint a particular country—and sometimes a specific city— where the water in the sample came from.

A microbiologist tests a sample sent for anthrax testing in Montgomery, Alabama, in October 2001. This lab was behind because of the increase in samples requiring anthrax testing.

THE
DOWNLOAD

Here's even more amazing stuff about bioterrorism for you to read.

IN THIS SECTION:

- ► how the plague became the first bioweapon in 1347;
- ► how bioterrorism has been in the news;
- ► the tools experts use to catch bioterrorists;
- ► and whether microbiology might be in your future!

1347 Black Death

From 1347 to 1350, a deadly **bubonic plague** kills as many as 30 million people in Europe (*left*) and parts of Asia. Over the next 200 years, plague is used as a bioweapon. How? People and animals infected with plague are thrown into the water supplies of enemy towns.

Key Dates in Bioterror

When were bioweapons first used? It all began with the plague in the 1300s.

1754 Deadly Gifts

Smallpox is a deadly virus that has been used as a bioweapon. During the French and Indian War (1754–1763) colonists are said to have given smallpox-infested blankets to the Native Americans (*right*).

1914—1918 Germans Use Nerve Gas

During World War I (1914–1918), German scientists develop weapons like anthrax to kill cows, sheep, and other livestock. Later in the war, the Germans use mustard gas and other biological weapons against their enemies. The results are so terrible that, after the war, a treaty is developed to stop their use. The Geneva Protocol now prohibits the use of chemical and biological weapons during war.

1936–1945 World War II Bioterrorism

During World War II, the Japanese conquer parts of China. Starting in 1936, Japanese scientists experiment on Chinese prisoners to find the most deadly forms of anthrax, **cholera**, and plague. As many as 10,000 Chinese are killed. The Japanese also drop paper bags filled with plague-infested fleas over Chinese cities.

1988 Saddam's Evil Empire

The Iraq army, led by Saddam Hussein, uses deadly sarin gas in attacks against its own people in the city of Halabja. An estimated 5,000 people die.

1995 The Subway Slayings

A Japanese religious cult called Aum Shinrikyo releases poisonous sarin gas in five different Tokyo subway lines. Many people are made sick, and 12 die. Cult members, including Shoko Asahara (*right*), are convicted and sentenced to death for this act.

See Case #1.

2001 Deadly Anthrax Attacks

Letters containing deadly anthrax powder are sent to members of the news media (*left*) and U.S. Congress. More than 20 people are infected and five die.

Tom Brokaw
NBC TV
30 Rockefeller Plaza
New York NY 10112

See Case #3.

THE DOWNLOAD FLASHBACK

45

In the News

U.S. Approves Project BioShield

WASHINGTON, D.C.—July 21, 2004

To defend America against bioterrorism, U.S. President George W. Bush signed a new law called Project BioShield. It gives $5.6 billion to develop vaccines against anthrax, smallpox, and other deadly germs. Some 75 million doses of anthrax vaccine will be made.

Scientists will also be hired to study the best ways to defend the U.S. against chemical and biological attacks. "We know that if terrorists acquire chemical, biological, or nuclear weapons, they will use them to cause even greater harm," Bush said. "Project BioShield will help America develop cutting-edge defenses against catastrophic attack."

U.S. President George W. Bush signed the BioShield legislation on July 21, 2004.

Alan Green, a police officer in Manchester, England, speaks to the press about an anti-terror raid in the area. Green explained that the raid was related to the discovery of deadly ricin in an apartment in London.

Six Arrested; Deadly Ricin Found!

LONDON, ENGLAND—February 2, 2004

Six people were arrested by anti-terrorism police in Great Britain. The five men and one woman are connected to the discovery of **ricin** in London. Ricin is a fatal poison made from a kind of beans called castor beans.

The suspected terrorists have been charged with producing chemical weapons.

The group may have been planning to put ricin into an aerosol spray. That would be extremely dangerous, says bioterror expert Andy Oppenheimer. He also adds that would be extremely difficult—even unlikely.

Bioterror Safety: A Guide

It's not all out of your control. Here are four steps to getting prepared for disaster.

FIND OUT WHAT THE DISASTER RISKS ARE IN YOUR AREA.

Ask your local emergency management, health department, or Red Cross chapter:

▲ what types of disasters are likely to happen and how to prepare for each;

▲ what your community's warning signals sound like and what to do if you hear them;

▲ how you can help the elderly and people with special needs.

CREATE A FAMILY DISASTER PLAN

Have a plan in case you are separated.

(A) Choose a place outside your neighborhood in case you cannot go home.

(B) Choose someone out of town to be your family contact. Each family member and any babysitter must know the address and phone for A and B.

▲ Make sure all family members have identification with them at all times. Make sure they have the emergency numbers, too.

▲ Plan what to do if you are asked to evacuate.

▲ Plan how to take care of your pets.

If you are told to evacuate, take these steps:

▲ Leave right away if told to do so.

▲ Listen to your battery-powered radio for instructions from local officials.

▲ Wear protective clothing and shoes.

▲ Shut off water, gas, and electricity if told to do so.

▲ Leave a note telling when you left and where you are going.

▲ Call your family contact to tell him or her where you are going.

▲ Take your Family Emergency Supplies (listed below).

PRACTICE AND MAINTAIN YOUR PLAN

Every month: Test your smoke alarms.

Every six months: Go over the family disaster plan and do escape drills. Replace stored food and water.

Every year: Replace the batteries in smoke alarms.

EMERGENCY SUPPLIES LIST

▲ Signal flare

▲ Map of the area and important phone numbers

▲ Special items for infants and the elderly (diapers, formula, medication)

▲ Three gallons (11.4 l) of water per person

▲ Seven-day supply of ready-to-eat canned or packaged food

▲ Manual can opener

▲ Paper cups, plates, and plastic utensils

▲ Blankets or sleeping bags

▲ Toiletries (10-day supply of prescription medications, hand sanitizer)

▲ Cell phone batteries and/or phone charger

▲ A change of clothing, rain gear, and sturdy shoes for each family member

Put these supplies in an easy-to-carry waterproof container:

▲ Battery-powered radio, flashlight, and extra batteries

▲ First aid kit and manual and prescription medications

▲ Credit card and cash

▲ Personal identification

▲ An extra set of car keys

▲ An extra pair of eyeglasses

▲ Matches in a waterproof container

COMPLETE THIS CHECKLIST (YOU AND YOUR PARENTS)

☐ Put emergency phone numbers by each phone.

☐ Find out how and when to turn off the utilities.

☐ Do a hunt for items that can move, fall, break, or cause a fire.

☐ Stock enough emergency supplies to last seven days (see list at bottom right).

☐ Take a Red Cross first aid and CPR class.

☐ Find safe places in your home for each type of disaster.

3

The Bioterror Expert's Toolbox

Here are some tools and equipment used by bioterror experts.

microscopes and slides

Microscopes magnify viruses, bacteria, and other things that can't be seen with the naked eye. Scientists put samples on thin pieces of glass called slides. They put the slides under the microscope.

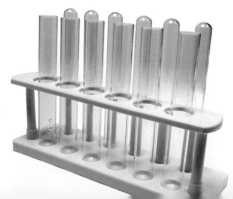

petri dish

Scientists use a petri dish to grow viruses and bacteria. They put agar, a kind of food for bacteria, into these dishes. Then they add the bacteria they want to grow. Soon, they have plenty of the bacteria to study.

test tubes

Bioterror experts use these long glass tubes to collect samples from the field. They also use them to mix chemicals and do various tests in the lab.

swabs Experts use cotton, rayon, and polyester swabs to collect samples of bioterror material. Then they test the materials to find out what type they are.

gene chip Bacteria and viruses grow from microscopic biological material called genes. Scientists put tiny strands of these genes on slides and study them. This lets them understand how different bacteria or viruses grow. It also helps them develop vaccines to protect humans against deadly viruses like smallpox.

mass spectrometer Scientists use this complex machine to study the differences between various biological and chemical materials.

masks One way to avoid inhaling dangerous bacteria or chemicals is to wear a mask. The best ones are called N-95 respirators.

biohazard suit Bioweapons can make people sick if they touch or inhale them. Biohazard suits protect scientists from getting deadly bacteria or chemicals on their skin. The suits also provide clean air.

HELP WANTED:
Microbiologist

Are you interested in studying bioweapons and microbiology? Here's more information about the field.

Q&A: DR. HELEN KREUZER

Dr. Helen Kreuzer is a microforensics researcher at the Pacific Northwest National Laboratories in Richland, Washington.

24/7: What's microforensics, exactly?

DR. KREUZER: It means using microbiology to solve crimes. The phrase didn't really exist until the 2001 anthrax case. A lot has happened since then.

24/7: What makes the best bioweapons?

KREUZER: It depends on what bioterrorists are trying to do. Anthrax is fairly easy to make, but it's not contagious. It doesn't spread from person to person. So it's like a bomb—it explodes and it's over. But smallpox is so contagious that it could start an **epidemic** that spreads around the world.

24/7: Is it hard to create bioweapons?

KREUZER: Some are harder than others. It also depends on how much you need. It's hard to make a large amount of anthrax!

24/7: **Can you explain how microforensics was used in the 2001 anthrax case?**

KREUZER: It's complicated. But here's one example: There's a rare oxygen **isotope** called oxygen 18. (An "isotope" is one of several different forms of an element.) Oxygen 18 is found in varying amounts in lakes, rivers, and water supplies across the nation. By testing the anthrax, you can pinpoint the water that was used to create it—and maybe find the place it came from. That could lead you to the criminal.

24/7: **That sounds like *CSI*. What kind of skills do you need to work in a microforensics lab?**

KREUZER: You need a basic science background. You need to understand what chemical formulas mean, and how to make chemical solutions. You also need basic math skills because we do calculations all the time. It's also important to take good notes, to communicate well with others, and to be a hardworking part of the lab team!

THE STATS:

DAY JOB: Microbiologists usually work in one of these four types of places:
▶ private labs, such as those at drug companies;
▶ universities, where they do research and teach;
▶ government labs, like the CDC or the National Institutes of Health;
▶ independent research labs funded by grants.

MONEY: The average salary for a microbiologist is about $70,000. But they can make more or less, depending where they work and how long they've been there.

EDUCATION: Microbiologists can have different levels of schooling:
▶ a PhD (at least 4 years of graduate school) is needed for advanced research
▶ an MS (at least 2 years of graduate school) is needed for basic research
▶ a BA (4 years of college) is needed for non-research jobs

NUMBERS: There are about 77,000 biologists working in the U.S. The number grows every year.

DO YOU HAVE WHAT IT TAKES?

Take this totally unscientific quiz to find out if being a bioterror expert might be a good career for you.

1 Are you easily freaked out by being around scary diseases?
 a) I get to work around scary diseases? Cool!
 b) Kinda freaked, but I think I can handle it.
 c) Of course. Who isn't?

2 Would you like working with living things that are too small to see?
 a) Yeah! I love looking at things under a microscope.
 b) Sure, but I'd like to get out of the lab sometimes.
 c) Nope. My favorite living thing is my dog!

3 Are you able to finish very difficult homework?
 a) Yes. I'm almost always done before my classmates.
 b) If I'm interested, I always get my homework done.
 c) I have to do hard homework? Forget it!

4 Do you love science?
 a) Are you kidding? I've memorized the periodic table!
 b) I like to watch *CSI* on TV. Does that count?
 c) I'd rather go to the dentist than do science!

5 Are you fascinated by how the human body works?
 a) I read everything I can find about the human body.
 b) Um, I think it's sort of interesting.
 c) Yuck! I'm afraid of blood and skeletons.

YOUR SCORE

Give yourself 3 points for every "**a**" you chose. Give yourself 2 points for every "**b**" you chose. Give yourself 1 point for every "**c**" you chose.

If you got **13–15 points**, you'd probably be a good bioterror expert.
If you got **10-12** points, bioterror investigation might be a good field for you.
If you got **5-9** points, you might want to look at another career!

HOW TO GET STARTED...NOW!

It's never too early to start working toward your goals.

GET AN EDUCATION

▶ Read the newspaper. Keep up with the news.

▶ Read anything else you find about microbiology. See the books and Web sites in the Resources section beginning on page 56.

▶ Spend time doing experiments (like the ones on Microworld.org).

▶ Take as many biology, zoology, botany, ecology, and chemistry courses as you can.

▶ Research colleges now. Start with their Web sites. Look for schools that have strong biology, zoology, and public health programs.

▶ Look into scholarships. Start with the BioQuip Undergraduate Scholarship.

▶ Graduate from high school!

NETWORK!

Find out if your community has a local biology lab. If it does, contact the director. Ask if you can spend a day learning about what he or she does.

GET AN INTERNSHIP

Get an internship with local companies, universities, or government agencies that deal with microbiology and bioterror. Contact the American Society for Microbiology for a brochure called "A Million and One." It tells all about careers in microbiology. You can get a free copy by e-mailing *fellowships-career information@asmusa.org* or by faxing your request to 202-942-9329.

LEARN ABOUT OTHERS JOBS IN SCIENCE

You may also be interested in these fields.

biologist: studies living organisms

ecologist: studies how organisms relate to the environment

entomologist: specializes in insects

epidemiologist: studies what causes, and how to control, epidemics

infectious disease specialist: studies illnesses that spread easily from person to person

parasitologist: studies parasites

pathologist: studies disease, especially its effects on body tissue

zoologist: specializes in animal life

55

Resources

Looking for more information? Here are some resources you don't want to miss!

PROFESSIONAL ORGANIZATIONS

American Society for Microbiology (ASM)
www.asm.org
1752 N Street NW
Washington, DC 20036-2904
PHONE: 202-737-3600

The ASM supports scientists who study bacteria, viruses, and other microbes. Anyone with at least a bachelor's degree in microbiology or a related science can join.

Centers for Disease Control and Prevention (CDC)
www.cdc.gov
1600 Clifton Road
Atlanta, GA 30333
PHONE: 800-311-3435

The CDC was founded in 1946, primarily to fight malaria. It is part of the Department of Health and Human Services. Today, the group is a leader in efforts to prevent and control disease, injuries, workplace hazards, and environmental and health threats.

Federal Bureau of Investigation (FBI)
www.fbi.gov
J. Edgar Hoover Building
935 Pennsylvania Avenue, NW
Washington, DC 20535
PHONE: 202-324-3000

The FBI works to protect and defend the United States from terrorism and foreign threats. It also upholds the criminal laws of the United States and provides leadership for federal, state, and local law enforcement.

Infectious Diseases Society of America (IDSA)
www.idsociety.org
1300 Wilson Blvd., Suite 300
Arlington, VA 22209
PHONE: 703-299-0200?
FAX: 703-299-0204
E-MAIL: info@idsociety.org

The IDSA represents physicians, scientists, and other health care professionals who specialize in infectious diseases. The society's purpose is to improve the health of individuals, communities, and society by promoting excellence in patient care, education, research, public health, and prevention relating to infectious diseases.

National Institute of Allergy and Infectious Disease (NIAID)

www.niaid.nih.gov/
6610 Rockledge Drive, MSC 612
Bethesda, MD 20892-6612
PHONE: 301-496-5717

For more than 50 years, NIAID has conducted research that helps treat, prevent, and better understand infectious and other diseases. It is part of the National Institutes of Health.

WEB SITES

CDC: Emerency Preparedness and Response

www.bt.cdc.gov/bioterrorism

This is a great site for information about bioagents and how officials deal with them.

Crime Library

www.crimelibrary.com/terrorists_spies/spies/index.html

This section of the crime library has true stories about terrorists and other lawbreakers.

FBI Kids' Page

www.fbi.gov/fbikids.htm

You can play games and read tips and stories to learn more about the FBI.

FDA

www.fda.gov

This site provides the latest news in food safety.

MicrobeWorld

www.microbeworld.org

This awesome site includes experiments, weird science, interviews with microbiologists, and much more.

NOVA

www.pbs.org/wgbh/nova/bioterror

Learn more about bioterrorism at this site from the *NOVA* TV show.

CAREERS

American Society for Microbiology
www.asm.org/Education/
index.asp?bid=1272

Want to know more about a career in microbiology? Check out this site.

National Institute of Allergy and Infectious Diseases
www.niaid.nih.gov/biodefense/
about/careers.htm

At this site, you can find out more about a career in biodefense research.

BOOKS

Brands, Danielle A., and I. Edward Alcamo. *Salmonella*. Philadelphia: Chelsea House, 2006.

Dashefsky, H. Stephen. *Microbiology: High School Science Fair Experiments*. New York: TAB Books, 1995.

Decker, Janet. *Anthrax*. Philadelphia: Chelsea House, 2003.

Farrell, Jeanette. *Invisible Enemies: Stories of Infectious Disease*. New York: Farrar, Straus, Giroux, 2005.

Gay, Kathlyn. *Silent Death: The Threat of Chemical and Biological Terrorism*. Brookfield, Conn.: Twenty-First Century Books, 2001.

Hirschmann, Kris. *The Ebola Virus*. Detroit: Lucent Books/Thomson Gale, 2007.

Lovett, Sarah, Mary Sundstrum, and Beth Evans. *Extremely Weird Micro-Monsters*. Jackson, Tenn.: Davidson Title, 1996.

Payan, Gregory. *High-Tech Military Weapons: Chemical and Biological Weapons: Anthrax and Sarin*. Danbury, Conn.: Children's Press, 2000.

A

agar (AH-gur) *noun* a jelly-like material used to help study lab samples

analyzed (AN-uh-lyzd) *verb* studied carefully, in order to determine the nature of something

anthrax (AN-thrax) *noun* a bacterial disease that is spread by spores. It causes blisters, stomachaches, and diarrhea, and it can be fatal.

antibiotics (an-tih-bye-OT-iks) *noun* medicines that kill bacteria

B

bacteria (bak-TEER-ee-ah) *noun* tiny single-celled life-forms found in the air, soil, and water. Some bacteria are harmless; others can cause terrible diseases.

bioagent (BYE-oh-AY-junt) *noun* a dangerous substance such as a poison, germ, or nerve gas

bioterror (BYE-oh-TAIR-uhr) *noun* the practice of attacking with germs and other biological agents to harm people and frighten others

biowarrior (BYE-oh-WAR-ee-ur) *noun* a person who combats bioterror

bioweapon (BYE-oh-WEH-puhn) *noun* a weapon that kills or injures through the use of poisons, germs, or nerve gas

bubonic plague (byoo-BOHN-ik playg) *noun* an often-fatal disease that is spread by fleas that live on rodents. Infected people can also spread it through coughing.

C

CDC (SEE-dee-see) *noun* a U.S. government agency that studies infectious diseases. It's short for the *Centers for Disease Control and Prevention*.

cholera (KAH-luh-ruh) *noun* a disease that affects humans and animals and is marked by diarrhea and other intestinal problems

civilians (si-VIL-yuhnz) *noun* people who are not members of the armed forces; ordinary citizens

contamination (kun-tam-uh-NAY-shun) *noun* the state of being unclean, spoiled, or ruined

Dictionary

cult (kult) *noun* a group of people with an extreme commitment to a particular cause

D

DNA (dee-en-AYE) *noun* tiny bits of living matter that tell life-forms how to grow and reproduce; the DNA for each living thing is unique.

E

Ebola (ee-BOH-lah) *noun* a highly contagious infectious disease caused by an airborne virus. It was first noticed in Africa in the 1970s. Symptoms include muscle and joint pain, fever, organ failure, and heavy bleeding. It is almost always fatal.

epidemic (ep-uh-DEM-ik) *noun* an outbreak of disease that spreads quickly over a wide area and to many people

evacuated (ee-VAK-yoo-AY-tid) *verb* cleared of all people, usually for safety reasons

F

FBI (ef-bee-EYE) *noun* the federal agency that investigates terrorism and other criminal activities. It's short for *Federal Bureau of Investigation*.

FDA (ef-dee-AYE) *noun* the U.S. government agency responsible for the safety of all foods, drugs, vaccines, and medical devices. It's short for *Food and Drug Administration*.

I

isotope (EYE-suh-tope) *noun* one of several forms of an element

M

microbiology (MYE-kro-bye-OL-uh-jee) *noun* the study of living things too small to be seen without a microscope

microforensics (MYE-kroh-fuh-REN-ziks) *noun* the study of tiny bits of evidence to solve a crime or unravel a mystery

N

nerve gas (nurv gahs) *noun* a gas that attacks the human nervous system

O

outbreak (out-BRAKE) *noun* the spread of disease in a short period of time and in a limited population (like a neighborhood, community, school, or hospital)

P

pesticides (PESS-tuh-sydz) *noun* chemicals that kill pests

profilers (PROH-fye-lurz) *noun* law enforcement experts who study past crimes to figure out who may have committed new ones

R

ricin (RYE-sin) *noun* a deadly poison made from castor beans

S

salmonella (SAL-muh-nel-uh) *noun* a bacteria found in uncooked foods like eggs and chicken. It can cause stomachaches and nausea but is rarely fatal.

sarin (SAHR-un) *noun* a dangerous chemical that is human-made and is similar to a pesticide

smallpox (SMAWL-pox) *noun* a deadly virus that spreads by contact. Up to 35% of people who catch smallpox die from it.

spores (spohrz) *noun* tiny, microscopic organisms that can reproduce

T

terrorism (TAIR-uhr-ih-zuhm) *noun* an act of violence against people for the purpose of creating confusion and fear. It's often used to protest a country's politics.

tularemia (too-lah-REE-mee-uh) *noun* a disease that is caused by tick bites and affects the lungs. About 5% of people who are infected die from it.

typhoid fever (TYE-foyd FEE-vur) *noun* a disease marked by fever, diarrhea, and intestinal problems

V

vaccine (vak-SEEN) *noun* an injection given to prevent a specific illness. It's usually made from a very weakened version of the disease so the body can learn to fight it off.

virus (VYE-ruhs) *noun* a tiny substance that can cause disease

W

WMD (DUH-bul-yoo-em-dee) *noun* bioweapons like nerve gas or anthrax that can kill many people at once. It's short for *weapons of mass destruction*.

Index

agar, *34*, 42
agents, 12, 37, 38, 39
Al Qaeda terrorist group, 36
American Society for Microbiology, 55
Antelope, Oregon, 32
anthrax, 10–11, *10*, 23, 36–38, *37*, 39–40, *39*, *41*, *42*, 45, *45*, 46, 52, 53
Asahara, Shoko, 23, *23*, 24, *45*
Aum Shinrikyo cult, 22–23, *23*, 45

bacteria, 9, 10–11, 27, *27*, 28, *34*, 37, 38, 50, 51
Big Muddy ranch, 32
bioattacks, 19–20
biohazard suits, 21, *21*, 51, *51*
biologists, 55
BioQuip Undergraduate Scholarship, 55
bioterrorism, 9, 12, 19, 24, 31, 45, 46, 52
biowarriors, 9
bioweapons, 8, 18, 24, 38, 44, 46, 52
Brokaw, Tom, 39
Bush, George W., 38, 46, *46*

castor beans, 47
Centers for Disease Control and Prevention (CDC), 12, 31, 53
Chamberlain, Carla, 30
cholera, 45
Cipro (antibiotic), 36, 38
civilians, 9, 19
conclusions, 14, 23, 33, 40

The Dalles, Oregon, *26*, 27, 33
disaster plans, 48–49
DNA, 42

Ebola, 23
ecologists, 55
education, 53, 55
entomologists, 55
epidemiologists, 55
Erickson, Daniel, 27
evacuations, 20, 48
evidence, 12, 14, 22, 23, 33, 39

Family Emergency Supplies, 48, 49
Federal Bureau of Investigation (FBI), 8, 12, 37, 39, 40–41
Food and Drug Administration (FDA), 30
forensics experts, 21, 23
French and Indian War, 44

gas masks, 21, 51, *51*
gene chips, 51
Geneva Protocol, 44
Green, Alan, *47*

Halabja, Iraq, 18, 45
Hayashi, Ikuo, 16, 19
health officials, 12
Huden, Johanna, 36
Hussein, Saddam, 18, 45

infectious disease specialists, 55
internships, 55
Interpol, 12
isotopes, 53

Kreuzer, Helen, 52–53, *52*
Kunimatsu, Takaji, *24*

Labrousse, Art, 33
Lantana, Florida, 37, *37*
LeBreton, Karen, 32
Livengood, John, 31
London, England, 47
Luntgens, Dave, 27, 34
Luntgens, Sandy, 27

masks, 16, 21, 51, *51*
mass spectrometers, 51
Matsumoto, Japan, 21, 22

microbiology, 8, *27*, 42, 52–53, 55
microforensics experts, 12, 52–53
microscopes, 8, 42, 50, *50*
Mid-Columbia Medical Center, 27
"A Million and One" brochure, 55
mustard gas, 44

N-95 respirators, 51
National Institutes of Health, 53
Native Americans, 44
NBC Nightly News television show, 39
nerve gas, 8, 9, 23, 44
New York, New York, 36, *37*
New York Post newspaper, 36
Niimi, Tomomitsu, 16, 19

Oppenheimer, Andy, 47
Osho. *See* Rajneesh, Bhagwan Shree.
oxygen 18 isotope, 53

Pacific Northwest National Laboratories, 52
parasitologists, 55
pathologists, 55
Pentagon, 36
Persichini, Joseph, 40–41
petri dishes, 50, *50*
plague, 44, 45
prevention, 28
Proffitt, Sue, 34
profilers, 39
Project BioShield, 46

questions, 14, 21, 29, 38
quiz, 54

Rajneesh, Bhagwan Shree, 32, *32*, 33, 34
Rajneesh cult, 32, 33–34, *33*
ricin, 47

salaries, 53
salmonella, 10–11, *10*, 27–28, 29, 30–31, 32, 33, *34*
sarin, 10–11, *10*, 16, 18, 19–20, *19*, *20*, 21–22, *21*, 24, 45

scholarships, 55
September 11 attacks, 36
Shakey's Pizza restaurant, 27, 34
slides, 50
smallpox, 10–11, *10*, 44, 46, 51
spores, 8
Stevens, Robert, 37
swabs, 51, *51*

terrorism, 8
test tubes, 50, *50*
Tokyo, Japan, 16, *16*, *17*, 18, 19–20, *20*, 21, *22*, 24
tularemia, 33
typhoid fever, 33

United Nations, 18

vaccines, 9, 38, 46, 51
virologists, 12
viruses, 9, 10–11, 44, 50, 51

Wasco County, Oregon, *26*, 27, 29, 31, 32, 34
Washington, D.C., 36, *37*, 39
WMDs (weapons of mass destruction), 9
World Trade Center, 36
World War I, 44
World War II, 18, 38, 45

zoologists, 55

Bioterror is a frightening subject. The good news is that there have only been a handful of incidents, and a relatively small number of fatalities. Also, there are a lot of smart, brave people working to thwart the bioterrorists. These include the doctors, nurses, and health officials who treat the victims; the scientists and microforensics experts who study the bioweapons; and the FBI and other law enforcement agents who track down the terrorists—often before they can even launch their attacks.

ACKNOWLEDGMENTS

I'd like to thank the microbiologists and microforensics experts I spoke with while writing this book. In addition to Dr. Helen Kreuzer, whom you read about, I also talked with Dr. Randall Murch, who started the FBI's microforensics lab, and Dr. Abigail Salyers, who worked on the 2001 anthrax case.

CONTENT ADVISER: Steven Aftergood, Director of the Project on Government Secrecy, Federation of American Scientists

Photo Credits: Photographs © 2008: age fotostock/COMSTOCK Images: 51 bottom right; Alamy Images: 4 bottom, 8 (Hemera Technologies), cover (Frank Chmura), 14 top (image100), 1 left (Gabe Palmer); AP Images: 41 (Luis M. Alvarez), 29 (Ric Feld), 23 (Kyodo News), 42 (Dave Martin), 24 (Kazuyoshi Sako/Asahi Shimbun), 46 (Evan Vucci); Bridgeman Art Library International Ltd., London/New York/Private Collection: 44 top; Corbis Images: 45 top (Bettmann), 37 bottom, 39, 45 bottom (FBI), 6 top, 45 center (Georges de Keerle/Epix/Sygma), 34 (Ian Harwood/Ecoscene), 5 top, 22 (Noboru Hashimoto/Sygma), 19, 21 (Noboru Hashimoto/Tokyo Shimbun/Sygma), 33 (JP Laffont/Sygma), 20 (Nikkan Sport/Sygma), 3 (Varie/Alt); DK Images: 1 right; Getty Images: 35 (Manny Ceneta), 25 (David W. Hamilton), 44 bottom (MPI), 14 bottom (Paul J. Richards), 50 bottom (Stockbyte), 5; Index Stock Imagery: 16 (Jan Halaska), 27 (Jacob Halaska); JupiterImages: 5 center, 30 (Matthew Borkoski), 50 top (Tetra Images); NEWSCOM: 6, 58 (Natalie Caudill), 32 (ZUMA Archive); Pacific Northwest National Laboratory: 52; Photo Researchers, NY: 4 top, 10 top, 11 left (Scott Camazine), 50 center (Victor de Schwanberg), 10 center top, 11 left center (A. Barry Dowsett/CAMR), 10 center bottom, 11 right center (Kenneth Eward/BioGrafx), 10 bottom, 11 right (Eye of Sciene); Reuters/Howard Walker: 47; ShutterStock, Inc.: 1 center, 2 (Jason Aron), 51 top (Ultra Orto, S.A.); Superstock, Inc./Brand X: 15; The Image Works/SSPL: 51 bottom left. Maps by David Lindroth, Inc.